HEART WOOD

T0163913

HEART
WOOD

MARY LOGUE

Homebound Publications
Ensuring the mainstream isn't the only stream.

HOMEBOUND PUBLICATIONS
Ensuring the mainstream isn't the only stream

Postal Box 1442, Pawcatuck, Connecticut 06379-1442
www.homeboundpublications.com

© 2020 · Text by Mary Logue

Homebound Publications and its divisions support copyright. Copyright fuels creativity, encourages diverse voices, promotes free speech, and creates a vibrant culture. Thank you for buying an authorized edition of this book and for complying with copyright laws by not reproducing, scanning, or distributing any part of it in any form without permission. You are supporting writers and allowing Homebound Publications to continue to publish books for every reader.

Quantity sales. Special discounts are available on quantity purchases by corporations, associations, bookstores and others. For details, contact the publisher or visit wholesalers such as Ingram or Baker & Taylor.

ISBN · 9781947003781
First Edition
Front Cover Image © Greg Rosenke
Cover Designed by Leslie M. Browning

Printed in the United States of America
10 9 8 7 6 5 4 3 2 1

Homebound Publications is committed to ecological stewardship.
We greatly value the natural environment and invest in environmental conservation.

I also saw that there was an ocean of darkness and death, but an infinite ocean of light and love, which flowed over the ocean of darkness.
—George Fox, Founder of the Society of Friends

And listen: the wind has come.
Finally, it always does.
It will touch everything.
—William Stafford, *Smoke's Way*

CONTENTS

3   Ordinary

4   On the Earth

5   Still, Life

6   Birth

7   Center

8   Glowing

9   Held

10 Sun

11 Simple Breath

13 Courage

14 View

15 Fear of Flying

16 The Belly

17 Water

18 Tracks

19 Bed

20 Rain

21 Teaching

22 Leaves

23 Trying to Stay

24 So Much

25 Quaker Meeting

26 Sailing to Shiva

27 Whisper

28 Listen

29 House

30 Aubade

31 Mop

32 Pearl

33   Vastness

34   Swirls

35   Halting

36   Sway

37   Ocean

38   Healing

39   Quilting

40   The Tree

41   Roses

42   Vine

43   Lunar Eclipse at the Winter Solstice

44   Dozing

45   Message

46   Instructions for Dusk

47   Wicks

48   Sprung

49   Unwinding

50   Last

51   Ash

52   Long Winter

53   Sitting

54   Why I Live in Stockholm, WI

55   Wabi Sabi

57   Plein Air

58   Flooding

59   Release

60   The Order of Things

61   Tales

62   Wasps

63   Verbena

65   Published Poems

66   Dedications

67   About the Author

ORDINARY

Any ordinary day contains a chance of whimsy,
the usual things can turn so that even getting
out of bed becomes an adventure. Remember

the slippers are two wool rafts bobbing
on the ocean of the floor. Try to stay upright.
Determine to move forward. Know that tap water

is an endless stream that flows through your hands
all your life. The walk you take so
the dogs can pee on someone else's grass

is the walk you are still taking since that first
time you fell forward and caught yourself
by putting a foot out, the next day

you ran away and you've been running
ever since, because that's all this life is
and there's no such thing as an ordinary

day, only pearls in a necklace of
devised divisions that mark sun, no sun,
moon, no moon, breath, no breath.

ON THE EARTH

That first rose light
that tips the trees,
no matter how bad
the night has been, promises

that all will be well
with the land, the eternal
clock of god's heart beat
will never stop and we will

always feel it close
if we stay quiet for a moment
and stand on the earth.

STILL, LIFE

The white shell sits still.
Life that was once, gone,

but the hard form,
the curves, remain.

Behind the shell,
another white,

more blue as if a touch
of sky has streaked it.

The opening of the shell,
a welcome door.

You know if you put your ear
to it what you will hear—

the sea moans
in all of us.

BIRTH

Perched next to your ear, the baby monitor catches
any sharp movement, any change in sound.

Hearing a moan, you throw on clothes,
trudge to the barn and find it warm with hay and wool.

You kneel, work to show the animal what has been bred out of it.
Your hand slides up the canal to find smooth hooves.

Pull and relax, the thrusts soon
have the new baby diving into your arms,

wet bundle of fur and curl, hungry for all the sweetness
it can mouth, ready to stand on its own four feet and totter forward.

Still on your knees, you worship this splitting moment:
Where there was empty air, there is now lamb.

CENTER

When sadness presses on me,
when sleep is stolen away,
what is left?

I stand next to a spring hackberry,
not quite as tall as the tree,
and watch its fuzzy leaves unfurl.

What is left is the sprout
inside the seed
deep in the heart of my wood.

GLOWING

Let's say this is it—
all we will ever know—
pages turning in the next room,
light in the clouds all around us,
dark pierced with stars,
one hand on another,
the soft taste of pear,
a singular body wading through air,
voices calling names,
that this is it, this world we
inhabit for a glowing time.

But let's say this isn't it—
what would we do differently?

HELD

I cradle the child in the water,
soft limbs, green bones,
her head on my shoulder.

Stretching her flat, I whisper:
Head back, belly up, arms out.
It will hold you.

I keep a hand tucked
into the small of her back
as she tests the truth of my words,

the strength of this liquid she drinks,
splashes through,
sprinkles on flowers,

to have faith that it can lift
every ounce of her up
to the sky like an offering.

Slowly I pull my hand away.
Her eyes widen
in wonder.

SUN

All summer long the lazy sun
meanders across the sky,
but as winter looms
it withdraws to the edge

of the world, crawling along
the horizon for a few short hours,
and we yearn for it as we hope
a lover will return from a journey

full of green gifts and growing,
again going to the center of our world
and holding our heads
for hours with benedictions.

SIMPLE BREATH

What is it that
keeps me from taking a full
breath, basic stitch
that holds us in the world,

this pulse, this beat,
this gasp of air,
why would I not take this in

to the fullest? One night
I woke in the middle, stars
pressed against the window,

fear filled me up from my feet
to my eyes.

I stood next to my bed
in my nightgown
and asked, "What are you

so afraid of?" Peeling layers
of knowledge and subterfuge away,
I thought, "I'm afraid

I'll see how awful we are
to each other and ourselves
and I won't be able

to stand it." There it was —
the worst that could be.
Now breathe. Know the worst

and breathe through it. Take
the whole world into your lungs,
every last fleck of it,

and fill yourself full of
shoes, noodles, and waves,
twigs, toenails and cups,

all the promises, all
the complaints, every last
thought that anyone could think.

Know how bad it can be
and how good.
Inseparable.

COURAGE

To be full of heart
means to rip open
a bit,
that vulnerability
where the world
leaks in:
rose petals,
flare of tear,
sorrow of
dead branch,
hung head,
dusty feet,
walking.

To be full
of heart
means to
pinch shut
that hole
when you
must
and say,
it doesn't hurt
much,
I can
still
do it.

VIEW

When you're a kid
no one tells you
that as you age
and pieces of you start
to fall apart—knees,
bladder, hair, heart—
there is one thing you gain:
The panoramic view
on top of all those years.

FEAR OF FLYING

When the land is large and flat
as a hand that could rise up
and whack you if the plane

you are in starts to fall,
when you sit in your tiny seat
next to the window and watch

the fields flow by and know
that if something goes wrong
that little cup that drops out

of the ceiling will not act as a parachute
and the seat cushion will not
soften your fall, that if the plane

aims toward the earth, the plane
won't win and you can either
crouch in your seat whimpering

with closed eyes or you could open them wider,
take in all the dusky light
you possibly can, watch the air whiz by

at infinite miles an hour
and put your hand to your heart
to feel every last beat.

THE BELLY

The navel is our epicenter,
the port through which we received

our first love—a mix of
warm blood and gentle touch.

If you try to attain that radiant
feast again, all you get is snatches.

Put your hands over your belly.
It's an ocean that swells and falls.

While we can never go back
to what we had, we can bring it with us.

Goodness and mercy, lighter than air.

WATER

Enter the water to let go.
As you walk in up to your waist,

you will be held in a million
hands. None grasping.

Like sleeping on petals,
giving yourself to the water

is an act of redemption
and utter faith in the real.

Dive below the surface.
You will be washed clean, inside and out.

Remember we came out of the water.
Remember the feel of first air.

TRACKS

I settle into a life
that never settles, but sways.

I learn to sit with myself
and call leaves from the trees.

I talk to break the silence
of sorrow, to hold small joys.

I stroll down roads where
people have their own worries.

Each bite of food I eat brings a memory,
mother and father at opposite ends of the table.

All this on paper white as snow.
Bird tracks—fly away.

BED

Staying in bed after I wake
is one of my greatest pleasures.

Sun leaks light through curtain clouds.
I float as if on water, as if on air.

A stillness coats my body.
Soft hum of bees leaving the hive.

I won't stay too long.
I know when the moment

is right to throw back the covers
and welcome in morning.

RAIN

I ask for compassion
and a million sorrows pelt down on me.
With each drop I know a little more
what it is to feel broken.

TEACHING

I know next to nothing.
Let's start there.

I open a door.

We walk through
into a world that neither
of us has ever seen before.

You describe
branches holding sky,
rivers that flood fallow fields,
all the earth reaching out for life.

I nod. This I know too.

We build
with no idea what it will look
like when we're finished,
hoping for a rushing river,
or a tall tree,
or even the earth
so full of yearning
it overflows.

We are in this world
for such a short time.

We never know
until we're done
what we will make.

LEAVES

"in ways I can't make out." — Rilke

The maple still holds its leaves
but I know they will fall.

Let the night be filled
with scratchy worries,

these too will pass.
A wind will blow through,

another day will appear
like the guest

we've been waiting for,
and we will welcome it all.

TRYING TO STAY

The snow is trying to stay snow
but keeps sliding toward water.
Drips off the eaves tell the whole story.

It's simply at the point where it melts.
How we would love to be white,
crystalline, virginal. But instead

we fall as globular-shaped tears,
smearing down the front of a windshield.
Never the perfect, always the blop.

SO MUCH

Gently reach out to me and
I will cross the sky for you.

We will meet where the tree
stands taller than the stars.

I think love is like plowing
a field, slow and steady,

dropping seeds as you go.
When harvest comes

we'll wade deep into flowers.
We won't know what to do

with so much beauty
planted in our chests.

QUAKER MEETING

People settle on hard benches,
shoes squinch, a hearing aid whistles.
Snorts, whispers, coughs, a sniffle.
Heat shushes the room.

Quiet buoys me up.
I float in the breath of all.
Every cell loosening,
I let go again and again.

Slowly my skin zips off,
heavy coat at the end of day
sliding from my shoulders.

SAILING TO SHIVA

In sitting shiva, the stool is lowered
closer to the earth. Listen.

We all enter to leave this place.
When we come into a house of mourning
we bring boats to find the shore
of living again. Delicate boats

made from words that we string
together, armada of sorrows
we all feel, the missing what
holds us tight.

This boat is for my friend's father.
I send it sailing around the room.
It dips to touch the people
on the lowered stools.

It brings them galleys of comfort,
laughter like waves buoy us up.
We all fall through the water
and will rise to the surface.

WHISPER

"Why use bitter soup for healing,
when sweet water is everywhere?"
—Rumi

I learn to sit still,
to rest with myself.
All I hear is slight hum

of earth turning,
all I see is play
of sunset inside eyelids.

Did I not know that the inside
is the same as the outside, that
there is no dividing line?

When my skin disappears,
when my mind turns into
dancing leaves,

the world blows through me
like the whisper of a lover,
soft but insistent.

LISTEN

The quiet of winter is a gift
if you listen. The message

is not literal. Don't be silent
but flowing. Even under the ice

the river runs freely. The words
I write surface moments before

they light on paper.
If I thought about them

they would be too heavy.
Like moths in a draft

they would fall. I fall, too,
beside them. Like snow,

like wings. Like all good
moments they erase the ground

we think we walk on.

HOUSE

My house is just a box with holes
to see fields, roads, gravel,

tree branch, bird,
clouds, faintest prick of starlight,

spilled milk of galaxy.
Sometimes I travel that far.

Often I'm stuck in thoughts
that take me down and inward.

How to open up the windows,
the body, the mind, the heart to the world?

I practice by watching the chickadee
eat a seed. Crack it carefully.

AUBADE

Those early morning sounds—
furnace chugging like a distant train,
dogs whispering in second sleep,
Peter standing and clearing the night
out of his throat—are almost enough
to lure me out of bed.

MOP

The blue heron looks cold and annoyed.
Like an old mop stood in the corner

of the closet, its dusky feathers
bristle with damp and exhaustion.

It pretends not to see me.
I try not to stare so hard it will leave.

Both of us are struggling with early winter.
You have a choice, I say. You can go.

I know you will, but not at this moment.
Not with my cranky eyes holding you tight

to an island in an icy river.

PEARL

I try not to hold my fear in my hands
like a precious pearl.

Sometimes sitting is all I can do.

Let the world churn around me
as I sink into where I am.

VASTNESS

Look up. The trees hold heaven.
They channel into earth while reaching for the light.

The great vastness is bigger
than our minds can swallow.

Our hearts have a better chance.
They don't try to figure it out.

As a child I sat in trees
to learn their music.

Now I hear it everywhere,
through my whole body.

I open my pores to wars, weddings,
and I'm filled with exaltation and despair.

Yesterday I stood in the cold
and it pierced me.

SWIRLS

Snow turns the woods black and white
until a cardinal dashes red from tree to tree.

A lovely, long slit in the creek
is still burbling dark water.

Around the edges, ice forms
scrolls like galaxy swirls.

I stare into the water
and, for a moment, spin.

The woods surround me
and I invite the trees into my heart.

HALTING

Our old dog flinches at ghosts.
They loom over the sidewalk

as he makes his halting way home.
I flinch, too, at what I know will come.

Walking into the winter wind,
I wrap my arms over my chest,

then reach down and cradle the dog.
He needs to be comforted.

We turn and go into the warm house.
The end is never in sight, just the next step.

SWAY

When the darkness lifts
it isn't only light that filters

into the room. The tapping of the dogs'
toenails sounds like rain in the night.

Smell of toast comforts like a hand on forehead.
Let the senses awaken slowly.

Each moment should be unwrapped
gently as if it might end.

Don't push the dark away.
Don't pull the light in close.

Let them dance with each other.
Join the swaying of their forces

that show us again and again
there is no separation.

OCEAN

Sitting on a straight-back chair,
I hear an airplane hush the sky overhead.

I am surrounded by an ocean of warmth,
created by the breath of all friends around me.

Love grows in our bones like marrow.
We lift up our eyes and, in awe,

they fill with light.

HEALING

Healing starts with one drop
in a bucket. A big bucket.

Don't try to watch it fill.
Rather listen to the sound

of rain on a roof.
Be patient.

Sometimes standing still
mends many broken places.

Healing is a silk thread stitched
through a dark cloth slowly.

QUILTING

Sew a quilt that captures
all the fibers of life.

This task will take more time
than you will be given

as the quilt keeps unfolding,
old fabric in new hands,

needles flashing in and out,
snakes swimming in a river.

An object does not have to be complete
to be worth all the trouble,

a line interrupted can say just enough.

THE TREE

This tree you gave me
captured on paper in a frame
is massively alive.

Covered with glowing green moss,
it has pushed out of the ground for years.
In its branches I see embrace.

I want to stand so sturdy,
arms always open
to catch the sky.

ROSES

On our anniversary, you flew away
for work, left twelve red roses

towering on the table. All week they kept
me company. I ate in their shadow.

Crimson color flooded me as I passed
through the house. Not much smell,

faint hint of a past life growing in soil,
it was their hue that filled the air.

It spoke of old love,
grown for years in many earths.

Love that claims a color,
beaconed out into the world.

Love that stands tall
on a table and watches.

Love that resists absence.
You come home tomorrow.

VINE

My love for you has grown
too big for my heart. I feel
it in my hands like a vine.

I smell it riding the air like
wood smoke on a cold day.
You feed me what I need

even when I'm not hungry.
That constant feel of your body
stirring beside me is comfort.

Whether the universe is bigger
than we can bear or
small as a tear in an eye,

we are in it and with it.
We have walked long roads
together. Look, the horizon.

LUNAR ECLIPSE AT WINTER SOLSTICE

Before there was time to fear,
a crescent cupped the darkness

and grew until it was as big as
a bowl of a face, shimmering.

From this day forward, there will be more.
Hold out your hands and receive the light.

Underground flowers stir.
Grass remembers green.

Writing covers my desk with
tendrils and shoots unfurling.

Every day I walk toward the sun
and every day I return home.

DOZING

My dog sleeps on my legs
while I read books about
god and the universe and rain.

My dog, like a glowing fire,
radiates a furry light.
For him, I am couch, heating pad,
rub, good foundation.

As the sun comes in the window, we bask.
My dog sleeps on my legs,
I doze with a book in my hands.
The light shines on us and in us.

MESSAGE

The geese fly to water
in the frozen air. I walk

in the calmness of new snow.
It's hard to stay indoors

when the sun burnishes the land.
Keep noticing the sky.

Sometimes feathers, sometimes
blades. Neither will touch you.

So it is with the scent of hours.
Don't watch the clock.

It will tell you nothing but loss.
While the sun, as it sails westward,

shines a solid message:
continue, continue.

INSTRUCTIONS FOR DUSK

Twilight glows green
and the birds sing their last song,
fast and furious.

Drop your hands
and with them your worries.
Tilt your head back.

Look through the branches.
See that glint of candle in the sky
there all along, always above.

Watch the light
sail into those dark seas,
a skiff to put your hopes in.

WICKS

As the sun glows on the lip of the earth,
I light a candle—
flame found home.

~

I stare at the core of fire—
red heart beating
outside my body.

~

I have come to love candles.
Single crown of light
batting back the dark.

SPRUNG

As if a cold hand clamped down for long months,
then eased and light trickled in, or as if

the land was brown as ash
until a sprig of green shared the spectrum.

It's as if I was sleeping, running from all I could
never face, running forever, then I stopped

held out my hand and a bird landed,
the first thing I could feel in those long months.

As if spring kissed the whole of me
with all I had been missing.

UNWINDING

The shoulders of the bluffs are generous
with green, so is the comfort of the fields.

The universe unrolls with every step we take.
Like pollen, love sifts over everything.

The last yellow held in the willow leaves
turns my heart into a bird. My body

unwinds like a spool of thread when touched
in the right way. The moon walked with me tonight

as I headed toward home. Remember how it feels
to open a door for the first time, light breaks out.

Turn around as many times as you need
to finally see. Like a top you blur into a hum.

Keep unwrapping the present. Drink the cup of sun
the earth has handed you. There's more.

LAST

Still painting
on the beach
as night draws
curtains from clouds
you stand with brush
and pull in this scene.

I know this desire
deep in the pit
of the body to capture,
to continue, to hold
the last of the light,
not let it go
into the next
dark moment.

ASH

Down so many paths, sadly I have carried you—
my brother, my sister—to your graves.
How could you give me this task?
Yes, I'm either dumb or try in vain to speak to ash.
Since the fates swept you away from me,
one after another, all that was left
was the ancient work of burial.
Handed over like a gift.
Tears flow. You are forever taken.
Again and again I say: be well, brother, sister, fare well.

(after Anne Carson's translation of Catullus 101)

LONG WINTER

I write to sing in a slight voice:
the trees are still here under snow
and I know they have leaves
inside their branches.

SITTING

I wonder
if there is a tiny door
at the bottom of my soul
where I could empty out the ashes.

A rose light flickers
inside my forehead.
I sink into an emptiness
that has no sides.

Stillness is sweeter
for its rarity.

WHY I LIVE IN STOCKHOLM, WI

The blue bowl full of water
the postmistress puts out for the village dogs.

The tan man who mows my lawn
with the care of a lacemaker.

The river reminding me to catch
what passes before it disappears.

Always the trees, sheltering house,
birds, sweeping the air clean.

Dark dirt of my garden accepting
my hands into its deep generosity.

The light that is cupped in the folds
of the bluffs and grows golden.

When night comes in this small town,
we all sleep, deep in good company.

WABI SABI

"nothing lasts, nothing is finished, and nothing is perfect"
—Richard R. Powell

nothing lasts

seasons roll over one another,
a tumble of leaves, grass, snow

flowers falter,
much as we want to hold on to them—
clipping their stems just so,
freshening them with water—
they concentrate themselves,
move into a darker hue

I'd like to believe that love lasts
yet I know that it too comes in waves
pulls deep, then drops

we will melt away some day,
change form into dust

nothing is finished

the round solidness of the period
the deep feel of pressing pen to paper
a completed thought, but before
we even pull our hand away
more words push to be written

a child is born and becomes
a creature of this earth,
hands like strands in the sea of air

I am writing my life
when I die
the soil will continue
in ever-expanding
circles of earth, longings,
and cells

nothing is perfect

I like crooked,
to see the hand clutch and waver
as it grapples with the straight line,
human smudge on pure white paper

while I want to think my work
would finally be right,
perfect is not my goal

the off-center eye,
chipped pot, scuffed shoe
tell more

PLEIN AIR

To stand out in a field—
sun showering your shoulders,
grass washing up wave after wave
of song and sorrow,

birds flutter bits of punctuation,
trees crowd the sidelines,
beyond it all
the big broad mirror of the lake—

to take it in
and concentrate it down
to brush tip, to make
this fullness the size of hands,

requires the patience of a god,
the focus of an ant.

FLOODING

Snow peaks rise from the parking lot
across the street. The rivers are full
to flooding. Losses, like so much water,
are flowing through me.

Woodpecker hangs on the suet,
almost upside down as if giving in, too.
The land must be washed clean.
New soil carried in the sweep.

Sometimes the flood's inside of me,
sometimes I'm inside of it.

I know to go with the water
it will bring me
to the spot I need to be—
damp and shaken,

but fully alive.

RELEASE

I'm the kind of person
who walks wasps outside,
holding them gently on white tissues,
releasing them to air.
It makes me lighter.

That night in the kitchen,
washing the dishes of the meal
made by the man I love
who has fallen asleep on the couch,
I know the presence that had
found a home with me
was now flying away,
released once again
outside.

THE ORDER OF THINGS

We humans think we're top of the heap
on this sphere of scrap, know more,
are as close to the power as one can get.

We think we're higher than the animals, the grass.
Don't we know that we die as they do?
Our very tissue rolls in the fur of a fox

on the way down. Maybe it's our need to order
things, how we love to add *er* and *est*
to the end of words, how we simply understand

in the easiest of fashions: the largest
mammal, the smallest fish, a rock, an electron,
a mountain. We list and arrange them

as if this will give us dominion. But what if
the very nature of order
makes us less? Keeps us separate?

What if one night—sleeping under pines,
hugging the growing ground
as a lover—would show us our real place?

TALES

Fairy tales were lampposts,
pools of light on the path
I knew I needed to walk
to the promised land—adulthood—
where my life would have wings.

Now, older, it is the tale
of the nightingale that haunts me,
singing for all her worth
to cure the emperor,
while imprisoned
in a golden cage.

WASPS

I thought they were just visiting,
winging and winding
under the eaves of the roof,
small clouds of glinting air.

Until I noticed they were
all headed to a hole in the wall,
wasps above my head,
so quiet I never knew.

We shared the house for my stay.
I wrote at the desk as the wasps
flew in and out, to the trees, the lake,
back into darkness.

I was flying back into my life,
holes my parents left, embrace
of water, into light, back to darkness,
every time holding a little more.

VERBENA

Sitting by a glowing fire, I pour hot water
over fresh-picked verbena leaves—

ovate-shaped, prickle-skinned blade—
with winter still here, but not for long.

The water in my cup turns light green,
shantung silk, smells of grass, lemons.

The fire broods like the fading sun.
I drink this soft brew

and listen to a rich-throated
woman sing about Harlem on the radio.

Dark pressing, pressing on the windows
and not all is right with the world.

Hurricanes have battered the south
and today we learn an earthquake

has wiped out whole villages
on the other side of the earth.

But I drink my tea slowly,
knowing I must savor it,

that's my life's work,
to wring every last

drop of joy out
of this perfect

leaf-green tea,
fire dying daily.

Published Poems

Turtle Quarterly
"Fear of Flying"

Green Blade
"Instructions for Dusk"
"Trying to Stay"
"Center"
"Birth"

Friends Journal
"Quaker Meeting"
"Sitting"
"Whisper"

Yew Journal
"Sun"
"Tracks"

The Whistling Shade
"So Much"

Collegeville Institute
"Held"
"On the Earth"
"Water"
"Breathe"

Sister Arts Chapbook, Phipps Center for the Arts
"The Belly"

Sixteen of these poems were first published in the art book *Trees* illustrated by Dodie Logue. Many thanks to Collegeville at St. John's University for my time there working with Michael Dennis Browne.

Dedications

"Still, Life" was inspired by a painting by Dodie Logue

"Birth" was written for Gerd Kreij on her 70th birthday

"Held" was written after teaching swimming at Courage Center

"Sailing to Shiva" was written for Ilene Krug Mojsilov's father Murray's shiva

"Halting" was written for Rene, our toy poodle, 1994-2011

"Roses" for Peter

"Last" for Barbara McIlrath, intrepid painter

"Ash" for my siblings, Helen and Jamie

"Why I Live in Stockholm, WI" is for Sharon Stumpf and for Bill Stumpf too

"Plein Air" is for Dodie

"Verbena" is dedicated to our National Public Radio system

About the Author

New York Times-bestselling author Mary Logue has published mystery novels, poetry, non-fiction books, and many books for children. Her awards include a Minnesota Book Award, a Wisconsin Outstanding Achievement award and an Edgar nomination. Her poetry book, *Meticulous Attachment*, received a Midwest Booksellers honor award. Her picture book, *Sleep Like a Tiger*, won a Charlotte Zolotow honor, a Caldecott honor, and Best Picture Book award in Japan. Mary has also worked as an editor at Simon and Schuster, Graywolf Press and The Creative Company. She has taught in the writing programs at the University of Minnesota and Hamline University and written for the *New York Times*, *the Star Tribune*, and the *Village Voice*. She lives with writer Pete Hautman in Golden Valley, Minnesota, and Stockholm, Wisconsin.

HOMEBOUND PUBLICATIONS
POETRY OFFERINGS

———

IF YOU ENJOYED THIS TITLE, PLEASE CONSIDER
THESE COLLECTIONS FROM OURA POETIC LIBRARY:

Joy is the Thinnest Layer by Gunilla Norris

Ruminations at Twilight by L.M. Browning

Having Listened by Gary Whited

Four Blue Eggs by Amy Nawrocki

The Uncallused Hand by Walker Abel

Rolling Up the Sky by Linda Flaherty Haltmaier

Water, Rocks and Trees by James Scott Smith

To Look Out From by Dede Cummings

The School of Soft-Attention by Frank LaRue Owen

After Following by Burt Bradley

A Taste of Water and Stone by Jason Kirkey

Children to the Mountain by Gary Lindorff

Night, Mystery & Light by J.K. McDowell

Rooted & Risen by Timothy P. McLaughlin

Blood Moon by Andrew Jarvis

WWW.HOMEBOUNDPUBLICATIONS.COM
LOOK FOR OUR TITLES WHEREVER BOOKS ARE SOLD

HOMEBOUND PUBLICATIONS
Ensuring that the mainstream isn't the only stream.

AT HOMEBOUND PUBLICATIONS, we publish books written by independent voices for independent minds. Our books focus on a return to simplicity and balance, connection to the earth and each other, and the search for meaning and authenticity. We strive to ensure that the mainstream is not the only stream. In all our titles, our intention is to introduce new perspectives that will directly aid humankind in the trials we face at present as a global village.

WWW.HOMEBOUNDPUBLICATIONS.COM
LOOK FOR OUR TITLES WHEREVER BOOKS ARE SOLD

SINCE 2011

Printed in the USA
CPSIA information can be obtained
at www.ICGtesting.com
JSHW080006150824
68134JS00021B/2322